EMERGENCY!

NUCLEAR ACCIDENT

Angela Royston

ARCTURUS

This edition first published in 2011 by Arcturus Publishing

Distributed by Black Rabbit Books
P.O. Box 3263
Mankato
Minnesota MN 56002

Printed in China

Library of Congress Cataloging-in-Publication Data

Royston, Angela, 1945-
 Nuclear accident / Angela Royston.
    p. cm. -- (Emergency!)
 Includes index.
 ISBN 978-1-84837-954-1 (library binding)
 1. Nuclear reactor accidents--Juvenile literature. 2. Nuclear power plants--Accidents--Juvenile literature. I. Title.
 TK9152.R69 2012
 363.17'99--dc22

2011006643

Series concept: Alex Woolf
Editor and picture researcher: Alex Woolf
Designer: Ian Winton

Picture credits
Centers for Disease Control and Prevention's Public Health Image Library: 16.
Corbis: cover (Artyom Korotayev/epa), 4 (Roger Ressmeyer), 5 (Bettmann), 7 (Jean-Paul Pelissier/Reuters), 10–11 (Karen Kasmauski), 14 (Edwards Air Force Base—digital/Science Faction), 15 (Bettmann), 17 (Wally McNamee), 18 (Igor Kostin/Sygma), 19 (Gerd Ludwig), 21 (Anatoli Kliashchuk/Sygma), 22–23 (Steve Kaufman), 24 (Bettmann), 25 (Asahi Shimbum/Master Photo Syndication /Sygma), 26 (epa), 27 (STR/epa), 28 (Frederic Pitchal/Sygma), 29 (Gerd Ludwig).
Getty Images: 13 (Fox Photos/Hulton Archive).
Ryan, Padraic: 12.
Shutterstock: 6 (Gelpi), 8 (Steeve Roche), 20 (photocell).
TopFoto: 9 (Topham Picturepoint).

Every attempt has been made to clear copyright. Should there be any inadvertent omission, please apply to the publisher for rectification.

Supplier 03, Date 0411, Print Run 1050
SL001699US

Contents

Power to Destroy

An atom is the tiniest part of a single substance. Yet by splitting an atom, people have unleashed the most powerful forces they have ever created. The splitting of one atom causes the next atom to split, and so on. This is called a chain reaction.

Dangerous energy

In an atomic bomb, the chain reaction is uncontrolled. It releases devastating amounts of energy, mostly as intense heat, which can destroy whole cities. In a nuclear reactor, the chain reaction is slowed down to give a steady supply of energy.

The explosion of an atomic (or nuclear) bomb produces extreme heat and a huge cloud shaped like a mushroom.

First atomic bombs

During World War II, scientists raced to develop the first atomic bomb. The United States won the race. On August 6, 1945, a B-52 bomber dropped an atomic bomb on Hiroshima in Japan. No single explosion has killed so many people or destroyed so many buildings. Three days later, a second atomic bomb was dropped on Nagasaki. Japan surrendered six days later.

EYEWITNESS

When Hiroshima was bombed, fireman Yosaku Mikami was 1.2 miles (1.9 km) from where the bomb fell. "We heard many people swearing, screaming, shouting, asking for help.... We tried to carry them by their arms and legs and to place them onto the fire truck. But this was difficult because their skin was peeled off as we tried to move them. They were all heavily burned.... We carried the victims to the ... hospital."

Hiroshima Peace Cultural Center and NHK

AT-A-GLANCE

Of the 340,000 people who lived in Hiroshima:
- 130,000–150,000 died in the first 3 months
- 76,000 were injured
- thousands more were never found

The bomb destroyed nearly 70 percent of Hiroshima's buildings. Across the center of the city, almost nothing was left standing.

A Nuclear Reactor

A nuclear reactor produces a steady supply of energy—mostly heat. The heat is used mainly to generate electricity but also to power some submarines. Uranium is one of the easiest atoms to split. Uranium is mined from the ground and then processed. It is made into tiny pellets and put inside sealed tubes called fuel rods.

The reactor

Atoms in the fuel rods are split inside a strong tank called the core. Special rods control the power of the reaction. Pushing the control rods into the core slows down the reaction and can stop it. Cold water flows around the reactor. It takes in the heat and so stops the reactor getting too hot. In a nuclear power station the heated water is used to turn a turbine to generate electricity.

Nuclear power stations are usually built beside the sea or other large areas of water. This is because vast amounts of cold water are needed to keep the reactor cool.

SAVING THE ENVIRONMENT

A nuclear reaction produces radiation as well as heat. Radiation damages living things, but it cannot be seen, heard, or felt. An instrument called a Geiger counter is used to detect and measure radiation.

What can go wrong?

Most accidents occur when the core becomes overheated. A meltdown, when the core catches fire, is the worst kind of accident. Power stations have specially trained staff on hand to deal with accidents. As well as putting out the fire, they try to prevent radioactive particles escaping into the air and falling on the surrounding land.

SAVING LIVES

A protective suit stops radiation from getting inside the human body. Without it, a large dose of radiation would kill instantly, or cause radiation sickness that kills within days or weeks.

This special suit covers every part of the body and protects the wearer from radiation.

Windscale, 1957

Windscale in Cumberland (now Sellafield, Cumbria), UK, has many "firsts" to its name. It was the first plant producing fuel for Britain's first atomic bomb, and it was the site of Britain's first nuclear power station. In 1957, it was also responsible for Britain's first major nuclear accident.

Fire breaks out

On Thursday, October 10, one of the nuclear reactors, which had overheated, caught fire. Operators desperately tried to cool the reactor and stop the fire from spreading. Throughout the afternoon and evening the men used scaffolding poles to try to push the fuel rods out, but the fuel rods had twisted in the heat and it was hard to move them.

Many people who lived in the nearby village of Seascale worked at Windscale. Until the fire, most residents believed that the plant was safe.

EYEWITNESS

Tom Tuohy, Deputy General Manager, later said: "This was a blazing inferno, and we knew it was pushing [radioactive materials] up the chimney, and we didn't know what to do about it.... Mankind had not faced anything like this ever before."

Source: BBC documentary *Windscale: Britain's Biggest Nuclear Disaster, 2007*

Risky plan

During the night the operators pumped carbon dioxide into the core, but the fire just kept burning and its temperature kept rising. Then the reactor managers discussed a new plan. Should they pump water onto the fire? It might work, but it might cause an explosion. At 9 AM they decided to try it.

The fire, which broke out in a building that produced fuel for atom bombs, was not visible from outside. Here a helicopter checks the building for radiation just a week after the fire.

SAVING THE ENVIRONMENT
The nuclear reactors at Windscale were cooled by blowing cold air onto them. The heated air then escaped through a tall chimney. At the last moment filters were added to the tops of the chimneys to stop radioactive particles from escaping too. Without these filters, the Windscale fire could have been catastrophic.

Windscale: The Aftermath

Tom Tuohy watched anxiously as the water hoses were turned on. There was no explosion, but the fire continued to burn! Then he ordered that the cooling fans be turned off so that less air reached the fire. At last the fire began to die. It took until Saturday afternoon, however, before it was finally put out.

Fallout

Throughout the fire, some radioactive particles escaped through the filters in the chimney. From Thursday afternoon onward, the level of radiation in the surrounding countryside was much higher than usual. Large doses of radiation kill fast, but smaller doses can cause cancers many years later.

BREAKING NEWS

October 11, 1957, Windscale ... A fire broke out in one of the nuclear reactors at Windscale in Cumberland yesterday afternoon. According to an official spokesman, the situation is now under control and temperatures are starting to fall. Local people say they first realized something was wrong when 3,000 workers were sent home in the middle of last night's shift.

If cows graze on grass that is covered with radioactive particles, the radiation will spread through their bodies and into their milk.

Milk ban

The authorities were worried that the milk from cows near Windscale might be radioactive. Tests on October 12 showed that the milk collected within 2 miles (3.2 km) of the site was dangerous and it was poured into the sea. Later the ban was increased to 8 miles (13 km). However, vegetables growing in the same areas were sold and eaten.

FIFTY YEARS ON— AND COUNTING

After the fire the reactor was sealed to stop the radiation leaking into the environment. Since then, other parts of the power station, now called Sellafield, have gradually been closed down. It could take 100 years, however, before the site is safe, and the radioactive waste will remain dangerous for 250,000 years.

Chalk River, 1958

Bjarnie Paulson was sent to Chalk River Laboratories in Ontario, Canada, after a fire in one of the nuclear reactors. He was an expert in cleaning up radioactive pollution, but he did not realize that this job would ruin his life.

The fire

When one of the fuel rods had caught fire on May 24, 1958, a remote-controlled crane was used to remove it. The burning rod split and part of it fell to the ground. Immediately, radiation poured through the 12-story building. A team of workers put out the fire by dumping buckets of wet sand onto the burning uranium rod.

The nuclear reactor in Chalk River Laboratories is used to make radioactive chemicals for medical treatments, such as radiotherapy.

+ SAVING LIVES

When one man had finished with his protective suit, it was washed down before being passed on to the next man. The men were also scrubbed down in a special shower before being tested to make sure they carried no radiation.

Cleaning up

The building was still highly radioactive. Paulson was put in charge of 600 soldiers, who used mops and scrubbing brushes to clean up the site. Everyone involved in the accident and the cleanup wore protective suits, so the authorities were sure that no one had suffered any ill health. However, between 1964 and 1978, Paulson developed more than 40 different cancers, mostly on his face.

Technicians at work in the Chalk River Laboratories during the 1950s.

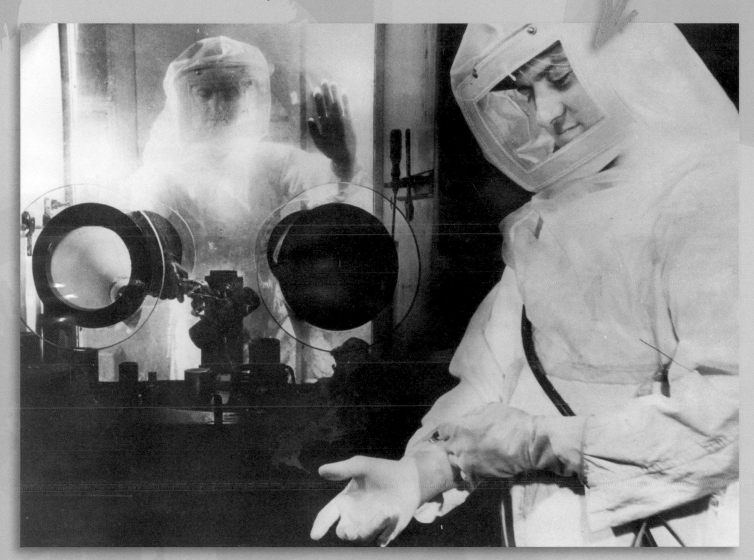

20 YEARS ON

Bjarnie Paulson realized that his cancers must all have been caused by his work at Chalk River and sued the authorities for compensation. At first the authorities claimed that Paulson had not been at Chalk River, but eventually they agreed to pay him a small pension.

Nuclear Bomb Accident, 1966

On the morning of January 17, 1966, in the skies over the coast of Spain, an American B-52 began to refuel in mid-air. The pilot had to fly very close to a larger plane carrying fuel, but he flew too close and the planes collided. The B-52 was carrying four atom bombs!

A military plane successfully refuels in mid-air by connecting up to a fuel plane. The operation takes great skill.

Mid-air crash

As the bomber split in two, the pilot and three of the seven-man crew parachuted to safety. Three of the bombs fell near the fishing village of Palomares. Although the bombs did not explode, the detonators on two of them did, spreading radiation over the surrounding land.

SAVING THE ENVIRONMENT

After the crash, farmland, woods and homes around Palomares were contaminated. The United States authorities removed 1,650 tons of radioactive soil and tomato plants and took them by ship to a nuclear dump in South Carolina.

Search for the lost bomb

A local fisherman saw the fourth bomb crash into the sea. People were worried that fish and the local beaches would be contaminated. The fisherman told the US Navy where to search the seabed. Even with the help of a small deep-sea submarine called *Alvin*, it took three months to find the bomb and bring it to the surface.

Spanish workmen near Palomares look at the wreckage of the B-52 bomber scattered over a hillside, as they assist in the search for an atomic weapon that was lost in the crash.

AT-A-GLANCE

In the 1960s there were 11 serious accidents involving nuclear weapons. In 1961, for example, a B-52 bomber carrying two atom bombs crashed at Goldsboro, North Carolina. All but one of the safety devices on one bomb failed! The bomb was 1,800 times more powerful than the one dropped on Hiroshima.

Three Mile Island, 1979

On Wednesday March 28, 1979, workers at Three Mile Island nuclear power station in Pennsylvania faced America's worst-ever nuclear accident. Part of the core of the nuclear reactor was in meltdown!

The fire

Early that morning, much of the water that cooled the reactor had accidentally drained out of the core. The core had overheated and the fuel rods melted. The fuel rods became so hot they produced hydrogen. The gas collected in the core and leaked into the building.

People living near Three Mile Island were alarmed and scared by the accident at the power station. They were worried about what might have happened.

Gas explosion

At 1:50 PM there was a loud bang—the hydrogen in the building had exploded! Operators in the control room were worried that the hydrogen in the reactor would explode too. For the next four days they struggled to gain control of the reactor.

Protest

Bit by bit, operators released the hydrogen and by Sunday, April 1, the danger was over. A small amount of radiation had leaked out, but no one had been killed or injured. Many people, however, now thought that nuclear power was too risky.

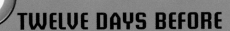

TWELVE DAYS BEFORE

A film called *The China Syndrome* had just been released. It was about a meltdown at a nuclear power station and it added to people's alarm at Three Mile Island. In the film a nuclear safety expert said that a total meltdown would make an area the size of Pennsylvania uninhabitable for ever.

SAVING LIVES AND ANIMALS

On March 30 the company that owned the plant discovered that radiation was leaking from the power station. People who lived within 5 miles (8 km) were ordered to leave the area. Farmers were told not to let their animals graze outdoors.

As news of the accident at Three Mile Island spread around the world, more and more people argued that new nuclear power stations should not be built.

Chernobyl, 1986

In the early hours of Saturday, April 26, 1986, one of the reactors in the nuclear power station at Chernobyl in Ukraine (then part of the former Soviet Union) went into total meltdown. Leonid Toptunov, an engineer, tried to push in the control rods to stop the nuclear reaction, but the rods jammed.

Fighting the blaze

The core exploded, and radioactive smoke poured into the air. Firefighters quickly arrived and tried to put out the fire by spraying water onto the burning roof. They had no protective clothing and many became sick and had to be taken to hospital.

Two firefighters, wearing protective clothing made of lead sheets, descend the roof of one of the reactors after the accident. Numerous firefighters have since lost their lives or have suffered severe health problems.

EYEWITNESS

Many firefighters died fighting the fire. Grigorii Khmel, the driver of one fire engine, described what happened: "We aimed the water at the top [of the building]. Then those boys who died went up to the roof.... They went up the ladder ... and I never saw them again."

Source: *The Legacy of Chernobyl* by Zhores Medvedev (W. W. Norton, 1992)

Burning core

It took only a few hours to put out the fire on the roof, but the core of the reactor continued to burn. Hundreds of helicopters were brought in to drop sack after sack of sand into the burning reactor. The sand contained lead and other chemicals. The authorities hoped that the sand and chemicals would stop radioactive particles rising into the air.

Nearly 20 years after the explosion at Chernobyl, an inspector visits the abandoned nuclear power station.

AT-A-GLANCE
- Immediate deaths: 31
- People with radiation sickness: 200
- UN predict total deaths will be 9,000
- People made homeless: 336,000
- Countries contaminated: 11

Chernobyl: The Fallout

Clouds of radioactive particles drifted from Chernobyl over the surrounding countryside. On Sunday, April 27, people were evacuated from the town of Pripyat. The authorities said that the move was temporary and so people left most of their belongings behind.

International alarm

On Monday, April 28, monitors in Sweden, 1,000 miles (1,600 km) away, detected a huge increase in radiation. At first the Soviet government denied that anything was wrong, but on Monday evening they admitted there had been an accident.

The town of Pripyat is still covered by a thick layer of radioactive dust. It is likely to remain a no-go area for 20,000 years.

BREAKING NEWS

Monday, April 28, 1986 ...
A radioactive cloud is spreading across Europe. It comes from a devastating fire at a nuclear power station at Chernobyl in the Soviet Union. The fire is still burning. So far, the cloud has put people in Sweden, Finland, and Poland at risk. Unless the direction of the wind changes, Germany and Britain could be affected.

The fallout spreads

A vast radioactive cloud spread across northern Europe. In Germany and other countries, the authorities destroyed milk and vegetables that were contaminated. On May 2 the cloud reached the Atlantic; heavy rain covered Wales and Ireland in radioactive particles. Sheep farms in particular were contaminated and the sale of sheep and their meat was banned.

Sealing off the reactor

It took until May 10 for the sand dumped on the reactor to put out the fire. Workers then built a thick shell of steel and concrete around the reactor to stop further radiation from escaping. Vehicles used to fight the fire, trees, soil, and other contaminated things were buried in huge pits that were lined with concrete.

24 YEARS ON

Most people who were evacuated from Pripyat have never been allowed to return to the town. Some sheep on Welsh farms still show signs of radioactivity from grazing on the hillsides.

This three-year-old boy from Belarus is suffering from thyroid cancer. Large areas of Ukraine, Belarus, and other nearby states were contaminated by fallout from Chernobyl.

Nuclear Accident at Sea, 1986

On October 3, 1986 a Soviet submarine carrying 16 nuclear missiles was on patrol 600 miles (1,000 km) northeast of Bermuda in the Atlantic Ocean. The submarine was powered by one of its two nuclear reactors. Just after 5:30 AM, an explosion in one of the missile tubes shook the ship.

Shutting down the reactor

The explosion killed three sailors and set fire to the missile tube. The submarine surfaced and Captain Britanov ordered that the nuclear reactor be shut down. Two sailors climbed down into the reactor chamber and for 30 minutes they tried unsuccessfully to lower the control rods by hand.

Trapped!

One of the sailors, Sergei Preminin, returned to the chamber and managed to shut down the reactor. The door to the chamber, however, had twisted in the heat and he could not open it. His comrades hammered on the door, but Preminin was trapped. He died in the chamber.

➕ SAVING AMERICA

Had the submarine's nuclear reactors exploded, a deadly cloud of radioactive particles would have covered much of the east coast of the United States. Thanks to his brave action, Preminin became known as "the man who saved America."

Nuclear-powered submarines have big advantages over conventional submarines. They can travel much longer distances without needing to resurface.

Defying orders

A Soviet freighter was sent to the area to tow the submarine and its crew back to the Soviet Union. Captain Britanov defied these orders. He evacuated the crew onto the freighter instead. Shortly afterward, on October 6, the submarine filled with water and sank.

AT-A-GLANCE

The United States, Britain, France, and Russia all have military submarines powered by nuclear reactors. There have been at least 14 known accidents involving nuclear submarines since 1961.

Tokaimura, 1999

On September 30, 1999, Japan's worst-ever nuclear accident occurred in a uranium-processing plant at Tokaimura. The reaction became critical, which means that it triggered an uncontrolled chain reaction, as in an atom bomb! The plant did not explode, but several workers were exposed to high levels of radiation.

BREAKING NEWS

September 30, 1999 ...

Reports are coming in of a serious nuclear accident at Tokaimura. Several workers from the nuclear plant have been taken to hospital. They are suffering from radiation sickness and doctors are fighting to save their lives. It is thought that the radiation has also spread beyond the plant.

Short cuts

The accident occurred because the company that owned the plant had introduced short cuts into the process of enriching the uranium. At about 10:30 AM, workers saw a blue flame rising from the fuel. As the radiation increased, the workers began to feel sick and alarms sounded in the building. Radiation in the building was 15,000 times higher than normal! Workers struggled to control the reaction.

Tokaimura enriches uranium fuel to make it easier to split the atoms. The fuel, in the form of pellets of enriched uranium, is used in research and in experimental reactors. Each of these pellets of enriched uranium contains the same energy as 1,780 pound (809 kg) of coal.

Clearing the area

Radiation outside the building was high, but not dangerously high. Five hours after the accident began, people within 1,160 feet (350 m) of the plant were told to leave their homes. After 12 hours, people within 6 miles (10 km) of the building were told to stay indoors. The workers added boric acid to the tank containing the uranium, and, 20 hours after the accident began, the reaction was finally brought under control.

Workers in protective suits help to transfer victims with radiation sickness to hospital.

AT-A-GLANCE

A total of 119 people were exposed to excess radiation. Of these, three workers were taken to the hospital. One of them died 12 weeks later and a second worker died 7 months later.

Fukushima, 2011

On March 11, 2011, a massive undersea earthquake in the northwestern Pacific sent a series of devastating tsunami waves crashing into the coast of Japan. Waves swept over the seawalls at Fukushima I nuclear power plant, destroying the power supply used to cool the reactors. Radiation began to leak from the plant.

Explosions and meltdowns

Shortly afterward, a series of explosions ripped through the buildings housing the reactors as the fuel rods overheated. A state of emergency was declared. On March 15, the authorities admitted that the cores of three of the four reactors had probably undergone partial meltdowns because of the high temperatures.

The Fukushima I nuclear plant in Japan. Each of the square buildings contains a reactor.

EYEWITNESS

On March 14, Hiroaki Koide, a senior reactor engineering specialist, said of the situation at Fukushima I: "We are on the brink. We are now facing the worst-case scenario.... If there is heavy melting inside the reactor, large amounts of radiation will most definitely be released."
Source: worldscenetoday.com

Radiation danger

Very high radiation levels were recorded at Fukushima I following the accident, and a number of people in and around the plant became ill. The government ordered the evacuation of residents within a 12.4-mile (20-km) radius. By March 15, radiation levels had reached 20 times the normal level in Tokyo, some 155 miles (250 km) to the south. Radioactive chemicals were detected in tap water in several cities.

SAVING THE ENVIRONMENT

Following the evacuation from the plant, 200 workers remained there, battling to reconnect the water supply in order to cool the reactors. They were joined by volunteer firefighters. The workers and volunteers risked death by exposure to radiation.

Evacuees living near Fukushima I nuclear plant are checked by medical personnel for exposure to radiation.

Can Nuclear Accidents be Prevented?

Nuclear reactors and radioactive materials are extremely dangerous. Those who work in the nuclear industry or with nuclear weapons usually take great care to avoid accidents.

Safety precautions

Strict rules govern everything to do with uranium, nuclear reactors, and nuclear weapons. For example, the core of the nuclear reactor in a power station is surrounded by a thick shell of concrete and steel. The shell should hold in any fire that may break out. Managers in a control room constantly monitor the nuclear reactor. They should see at once when something starts to go wrong. Nevertheless accidents do happen, often because people make mistakes.

SAVING THE ENVIRONMENT

Nuclear weapons, such as missiles and bombs, are often carried in bombers, submarines, and other vehicles. Nevertheless they are not likely to explode. Several safety procedures have to be followed before the nuclear part of them becomes active.

Government inspectors check the turbine of a nuclear power plant in Penly, France.

Public distrust

People fear nuclear accidents, not so much because of what *has* happened, but because of what *could* happen. Governments and the organizations that run nuclear plants do not want people to panic and so are often slow to admit there has been an accident. This makes many people distrust the authorities. However, independent organizations, such as Greenpeace, constantly monitor levels of radiation.

A Russian technician tests for radioactive waste from a nuclear processing plant near Sillamae on the Baltic Sea.

SAVING LIVES

The more nuclear power stations there are and the more countries that have nuclear weapons, the more chance there is of a disaster happening. The United Nations has inspectors who try to make sure that countries that build nuclear power stations do not use them to produce fuel for nuclear weapons.

Glossary

atom The smallest part of a pure substance. An atom consists of a nucleus, which contains particles called neutrons and protons, with smaller particles, called electrons, whizzing around it.

boric acid An acid that can be used to stop fire spreading.

carbon dioxide A gas that consists of carbon and oxygen combined. Carbon dioxide is often used to put out fires because it stops oxygen from reaching the flames.

chain reaction A reaction that keeps itself going. In a nuclear reaction, splitting one atom causes the next atom to be split, and so on.

compensation Money paid to make up for damage or loss.

contaminated Polluted.

cordoned off Describing an area to which access has been prevented by means of a barrier.

core The part of a nuclear reactor where the nuclear reaction takes place—that is, where the atoms are split to produce energy.

critical The point at which a nuclear reaction goes out of control.

detonator A small explosion that sets off a much larger explosion.

disposed of Got rid of.

energy Power, such as heat, electricity, light, and radiation.

enriching Making a chemical such as uranium more powerful or explosive.

evacuated Moved away from a dangerous area.

generate Produce.

hydrogen A colorless, odorless, highly explosive gas.

lead A metal through which radiation cannot pass.

meltdown An accident in a nuclear reactor in which the core of the reactor catches fire and melts through the protective materials surrounding it.

missiles Weapons in the form of rockets that are launched from one place to land on another place, often very far away. Missiles may or may not carry nuclear warheads.

monitor Check.

nuclear dump A place where radioactive materials are buried.

nuclear reactor A device that splits atoms in a controlled way to produce energy—mainly in the form of heat, but also radiation.

official Approved by the government or other authority.

pension Sum of money paid regularly to people who have been injured or have stopped working due to age.

radiation Rays produced by some materials, particularly uranium, as the nucleus breaks down.

radioactive particles Dust and smaller pieces of material that give off radiation.

reaction When a chemical substance is changed, for example by combining with another chemical substance. In a nuclear reaction, the nucleus of an atom is changed by splitting it.

remote-controlled Controlled from a distance, usually using radio waves or electricity.

Soviet Union A state encompassing Russia and other nearby countries, which existed from 1922 to 1991.

tsunami A long, high sea wave caused by an undersea earthquake or other disturbance.

turbine A machine that turns to generate electricity.

uranium A chemical substance that has the largest atoms found in nature. Uranium gives off radiation naturally.

uranium-processing plant A factory where uranium is enriched to make it easier to split the atoms. The uranium that is being enriched may be newly mined uranium or uranium that has already been used in a nuclear reactor.

Further Information

Books

The Chernobyl Nuclear Disaster by W. Scott Ingram (Facts on File, 2005)
Eye on Energy: Nuclear Power by Jill C. Wheeler (Checkerboard Books, 2007)
Meltdown: A Race Against Nuclear Disaster at Three Mile Island: A Reporter's Story by Wilborn Hampton (Candlewick, 2001)
Nuclear Accidents (Man-Made Disasters) by Mark Mayell (Lucent, 2003)

Web Sites

www.ccnr.org/paulson_legacy.html
Web site put up by the Canadian Coalition for Nuclear Responsibility, telling the story of the fire at Chalk River and Bjarnie Paulson's fight for compensation.

www.eia.doe.gov/kids/energy.cfm?page=nuclear_home-basics
Web site of the US Energy Information Administration: explains how nuclear energy works.

www.greenpeace.org/india/news/nuclear-nightmares
This web site relates the personal experience of one woman, who was five years old when the fire began at Chernobyl, not far from her home.

www.lakestay.co.uk/1957.htm
An account of the fire at Windscale and the reaction of local people.

www.world-nuclear.org/info/inf36.html
World Nuclear Association's web site, giving the facts about the accident at Three Mile Island.

Movies

The China Syndrome (1979) MPAA rating: PG
This is an exciting movie, but it is not accurate about what happens when a nuclear reactor catches fire.

Dr. Strangelove or: How I Learned to Stop Worrying and Love the Bomb (1964) MPAA rating: PG
This is a comedy with a serious message about how a nuclear war might be started by accident.

Too Hot to Handle (2010)
A three-part documentary TV series about the benefits and risks of nuclear energy, now available on DVD.

Index